Healthy Aging

Looking 20 in Your 50s
(Tips to Flourish Aging)

Smart Hijabi

DISCLAIMER

Copyright © 2024, by Smart Hijabi

TABLE OF CONTENTS

ABOUT THE BOOK

Healthy Aging offers a care routine and guidelines that will enable you to look outstanding at 20 in your 50s. Why should you lose that pretty/handsome look or well-built body and shape when you can still maintain it?

Unfortunately, the fear of aging(gerenotophobia) has caged many into losing their best self. And yet our society sees it as insignificant to educate on. Worry no more as this age-friendly book is here to ride you through the journey of Golden Years. Be ready to welcome the best version of you. A peruse for all.

ABOUT THE AUTHOR

Smart Hijabi is a nonfiction writer who creates top-notch content with her mind and pen to impact lives. She is interested in developing optimism in the mindset of her readers. Hijabi is the author of the book, Summary of Peace is Every Step. Smart Hijabi is known to observe her environment and curb negativity with her creativity.

INTRODUCTION

Over the years, I can't help but think why people worn out just because they are aging. Aging is a beautiful biological process and as such we should welcome it and be grateful. Many seek to age but a few are opportune.

Being optimistic and happy will ride you to lifelong growth.

Healthy Aging empowers the environments and opportunities that make people be and do what they desire throughout their existence

So remember, taking care of your well-being is crucial and such should not be taken for granted. You can become that person you have always wanted to be even as you grow old. Age is not a criterion for healthy living and success.

CHAPTER 1: What is Healthy Aging?

Every individual in the world can experience healthy aging. You don't need to acquire so much wealth to be healthy. It is said, our health is our wealth. You need health to acquire wealth and not the other way around.

Being free of illness or infirmity is not a requirement for aging. Many older people have one or more health challenges and when properly taken care of, have a slight effect on their health.

Have you ever had a cross of thought to ask yourself how well you are aging? Are you aging in the deserved right way? Or are you getting worn out each day?

What is aging?
Aging is defined as a biological process in which a person shows characteristics of increasing age. It is the total transition in a person over time.

What is healthy aging?
Healthy Aging is empowering the favorable environments and opportunities that ensure people be and do what they desire throughout their existence.

The society where we grow or live can have attributes on a person's behavior or well-being either positively or negatively. Environmental risks such as air pollution , violence, or noise pollution can affect our access to quality social and health care.

The World Health Organization (WHO) defines healthy aging as "the process of creating and preserving the functional ability that fosters wellbeing in older age".

What is Functional ability?
Functional ability is defined as having the ability that makes people to be and empower what they desire or value.
These abilities include:
- ☐ Ability to meet their basic needs

- ☐ Ability to learn, grow, and make decisions
- ☐ Ability to be mobile
- ☐ Ability to build and maintain a relationship
- ☐ Ability to contribute to the society

These abilities consist of the inherent capacity of the individual, relevant environmental features, and the relationship between the

Inherent capacity consists of all the cognitive and physical capacities that a person can draw on and these are the ability to walk, think, see, hear, and remember. The level of inherent capacity is influenced by various conditions which are the presence of diseases, injuries, and age-related change

The Environments comprise the home, community, and society, and all the factors within them which are the built environment, people and their relationships, attitudes and beliefs, health, and social policies, the systems that empower them, and the functions that they practice. Being able to live in environments that support and maintain one's intrinsic capacity and functional ability is important to healthy aging.

The different ways a person becomes old are:
- ☐ Chronological age: This refers solely to the order of time. That is, the years a person has spent in life….
- ☐ Biological age: This refers to transition in the body that commonly happens as a person age.
- ☐ Psychological age: This refers to how people respond to emotions.

In different societies, various terms are used in describing old persons, such as "the aged", "the elderly people", "older persons", "seniors", "senior citizens", and "older adults", only to mention a few. Presently, there exists no universally acceptable term for older persons.

Growing old should not call for fear, it is only natural to age. You know, you can not be in your prime forever. Many are not opportune to witness this beautiful stage in life and by chance, you are still breathing at 50 years and beyond. Why can't you be grateful to God and make your golden years count?

Fear no more, here are lots of tips to age and look young, beautifully/handsomely, and more admiring than your prime.

CHAPTER 2: Things to do when aging (promoting healthy aging)

Many people fear they will be a liability when they become old. While some think it is the perfect time to be totally dependent. Yes, you need to relax and seek help when necessary but you do not have to be too lazy and insist on doing some little things on your own. Make things easy for your caregivers and guardians.

Caring for your physical and mental health is significant for healthy aging. Making little changes in your routine can help you stay healthier and better. In general, you can help your physical health by staying dynamic, eating and resting well, and going to the doctor often.

Getting older is a process. And it can bring up a lot of emotions — for individuals, caregivers, and loved ones. But aging doesn't have to translate into self worthlessness and denial. Don't deprive yourself of happiness by leaving the beautiful good things you love doing. After all, your "golden years" are so named for a reason. Your 50s and beyond should serve as the best years of your life. Grab even the least of all and be fulfilled.

Making the most of life isn't just about living longer. It's about aging well. That means that we continue to enjoy a high quality of life as we grow older. Aging well depends on prioritizing our mental, physical, and emotional well-being.

Many of us find purpose in the day-to-day. We go to work, we care for our families, we learn new things, and we spend time with friends. But as we progress, we often have little or less of these responsibilities. As a result, we often feel somewhat absent. If our mental fitness routines were inspired by our outdoor work, we frequently let them slide. Engage in exercises, sleep, express gratitude and learn.

Mental Fitness and Aging

Although most conversations about mental well-being focus on mental health, it's not the only dimension of wellness. Mental fitness is about more than just "not being sick." It's about the skills and practices to sustain your most productive, resilient, and empowered self.

Mental fitness isn't one-size-fits-all. Your mind fitness practices help you strengthen and improve your cognitive and emotional health. You can engage in whatever makes you feel dynamic, attentive, at peace, or that awesome spot of "challenge" where you feel fully mindful. That might mean watercolor painting, doing crossword puzzles, playing with your grandchildren, making friends and hanging out, or starting a new vocation/business.

Our mental fitness practices can become specifically significant as we age. The cognitive decline that we tag with advanced age isn't unavoidable. Studies have shown that older persons are capable of doing – if not outperforming – younger adults on tasks. Strength can be found in older adults.

The following are routines to promote healthy aging:

Regular Moderate Exercise

Scientific Study has shown that regular and practiced exercise improves both physical and mental fitness. You don't have to do too many workouts at the rec center to exercise. Physical and simple exercises like jogging, walking, dancing, playing games, and word puzzles improve mindfulness and enable sound sleep.

You can decide to have a stroll with friends or family before lunchtime, regular exercise helps people age more slowly and live healthier, more vigorous lives. And it also helps people live longer. The more you work to stay dynamic as you age, the lower your chances are for things like high blood pressure, cardiovascular diseases, and stroke.

Amazingly, exercise boosts HDL ("good") cholesterol and lowers levels of LDL ("bad") cholesterol and triglycerides. And the same varieties of exercise will fight some of the neurological and psychological changes of aging. Endurance exercise boosts mood and improves sleep, countering nervousness and depression.

As simple as regular moderate exercise might look, it helps in cell growth thereby replacing old and damaged skin cells with new and healthy ones.

You, yes you, add exercise to your daily routine and thank me later.

Visit the doctor

It's always advisable to go for checkups often, but these check-ins become even more necessary as you get older. Visiting the doctor often can enable you to stay on top of your health. It can also help you forestall illness before it starts or prevent more critical illnesses early.

While you're at the doctor,ensure to tell them about any single worry you have - large or small. Don't be shy, to say the least of things. Keeping flow of communication open is a significant sign of being proactive about your well-being. Your doctor can recommend any screenings, supplements, or lifestyle changes that can benefit you.

Over the years, I have seen grannies regular and punctual at their checkups. At first, they feel hesitant to have a one-to-one meeting with a medical professional because they doubt themselves. They believe that they don't need any medical help because they are not sick. You don't need to be sick to have regular checkups. Checkups prevent unforeseen health issues and keep you on the right track to being healthy.
In due time they learn to open up to their physician. This progress improves the communication between them and their physician, also makes them feel safe, and say the least of worries.

Caregivers, guardians, and health practitioners assigned to older people should be friendly, welcoming, and helpful to enable a smooth transition with the aged.

Get plenty of sleep

Many of us overlook the significance of getting sufficient rest each night. Just one missed night of rest is associated with increased physical distress, more negative emotions, and less positive feelings. Despite myths that one needs less rest as you age, older people need 7 to 9 hours of sleep every night.

Whether you're retired or working, now is the time to start prioritizing your sleep schedule. If you're naturally a night owl, years of rising early might have you sleep-deprived. You may discover that feeling better rested might batten every aspect of your life.

The advantage of sound rest cannot be over-emphasized. Ensure to have enough rest to improve your health and look younger than your age.

Stay positive

A significant number of us anticipate retirement as an opportunity to at long last do what we like to do. Others, nonetheless, need time to change from (and to grieve) their working years.

Try to remain optimistic. Our society often discusses aging as a terrifying process. Be that as it may, it's an amazing season of life as well. Setting up and creating a growth mindset can assist you with checking out the conceivable outcomes in this next chapter of your life.

Here is a benefit of seniorhood: you have additional time, your children are on their own (grown-up), and you care less about what people process of you — especially if you have positive age convictions. Make a list of what you believe you should do and begin by doing it consistently without dawdling and faltering.

Healthy Aging

The prerequisite you need is to set your mind for it and most importantly be hopeful.

Connect with loved ones(friends and family)

Having cozy relationships isn't just about having somebody to sit in front of the television with. Our loved ones quantifiably affect our overall well-being. Investing energy and spending time with friends and family is shown to reduce the risk of hypertension, improve the immune system, and lower rates of depression.

Most old people think behaving or acting one's age means remaining disconnected and blending with just individuals of their age. This thought has pushed numerous to misery. Who said, because you are in your fifties or sixties you shouldn't have companions in their twenties.

Age they say is just however a number. Associate and spend time with whoever you need to.
You can be a mentor to the age coming up. Share your wealth of knowledge with them. Make some quiet memories in interaction as opposed to simply being detached.

Funny enough the way that some hold grudges with people. Purge your heart from anything that will occupy your inner serenity. Hard feelings are an entire interruption to oneself. Help yourself by remaining pleased with everybody until the end of your time.

Imagine you have this family or friend you have not been at peace with for some time and out of nowhere death comes dismissing the individual from the earth's surface.
Will you find a sense of contentment with yourself?
Will you whimper in lament?
Or on the other hand, would you have wished to settle your disparities and gain the best experiences before the takeoff?

Think wisely and gain the best experiences with everybody dear to you. You just know about this second, the next isn't guaranteed. Death, the unavoidable can come visiting.

I know of an old man who lived for a considerable length of time, 8 decades to be precise. There was something sad about him, he had no patience or tolerance towards people. He was nicknamed, " Mr. Perfect", constantly loathing and holding hard feelings against companions, neighbors, and family. There's no such word as "forgiveness" in his way of thinking. The fateful day he passed on, he was left with nobody to mourn him. It was as if no one was lost.
Try not to be that grouchy old man that passed on. Love, forgive, and be happy.

Learning a new thing

We should be optimistic about aging to continue to advance as we become old. It's about time we dismissed the familiar saying "You can't teach an old dog new tricks". On the off chance that you trust in this, hence you are saying you can't learn or are reluctant to attempt new things The tip to an enthusiastic old age is to accept you can learn new things even as you attain your 60s, 70s, 80s, 90s, and beyond— and recent research supports this.

Keep your brain dynamic and be hopeful (and perhaps uncover a new passion) by discovering and learning something new. It doesn't matter what new skills you seek, as long as you think that it is challenging and intriguing.

Even though there are no limitations on what you can decide to learn, it helps if the work is characteristically fulfilling. The more you enjoy the activity for its own sake, the more probable you are to encounter flow. A flow state is related to less tension, more good feelings, and a decreased level of anxiety.

What new things have you been learning as of late?

On the off chance that you are not eager to learn something new, would you say you are okay with missing the fun that comes with learning?

Do you feel comfortable forfeiting your capacity to learn?

Think about every person who doesn't take advantage of the web since they will not maximize the potential chance to know how to utilize it.

Do you truly want to pass up those things you have always wanted to learn?

Our body has a few constraints to age, however our mind is tremendous in its ability to learn and create. Carrying on with a life of consistent learning is fundamental. If you have any desire to be promising at understanding new things, then you should frequently leave your shell to learn.

All the old people I know who are vibrant and energetic are always eager to learn new stuff and teach it. And this is because they constantly learn and their brains stay active.

There is only one condition for lifelong learning: optimism - the belief that you can do it and that age is not a factor in learning.

As you grow, you either become your best version or your worst self. Choose wisely, no one is going to do that for you.

Eat healthy foods

It's no surprise that a balanced diet plays a significant role in staying healthy. What we consume translates into several areas of health, like cholesterol, our risk of heart disease, and our quality of life.

A healthful diet varies from individual to individual, and you should bring any specific concerns to your nutritionist. However, most experts agree that you should eat a well-rounded diet, complete with whole grains and fresh vegetables.

In particular, you should be sure to get enough calcium and vitamin D — whether from whole foods or a supplement. Calcium helps you to reduce the risk of osteoporosis and fractures. Low vitamin D levels are a risk factor for several health problems. These include cancer, heart disease, diabetes, high blood pressure, and cognitive decline.

Refill on fiber:

"Fiber is critical for helping with a healthy heart," Sauceda says. It has cholesterol-lowering effects. The other thing about fiber is that it will help with blood sugar.

If you are looking for foods to help you live longer and stay healthy, look for Fruits high in fiber.

What are those foods high in fiber? Fibers can be found in :

- Oats
- Fruits, Vegetables, Whole grain, Seeds and nuts such as raspberries, avocado, pear, apple, peas, grapefruit, persimmon, oranges, strawberries, blueberries, pomegranate, banana, kiwi fruit, passion fruit, dried fruits, prunes, popcorn, sweet potatoes, broccoli, okra, carrot, artichokes, chia seeds, flaxseed, chickpeas, millet, pearled barley.
- Legumes such as split peas, dried beans (red kidney beans, baked beans, lentils.

Fiber, which can be obtained from many plant-based foods helps you feel full. Fiber can also help with weight management, which is a common concern, particularly among postmenopausal women.

                                          Healthy Aging

•Add protein to snacks and meals

"Protein helps stop muscle loss, but many older people don't get enough",
Sauceda says.

It can take some work to consume more protein-rich foods since they aren't our regular grab-and-go snacks. Eggs, meat, and dairy products are sources of protein. So are plant-based foods like nuts, beans, and seeds. Protein plays a part in bone health. Getting enough protein is very important for women, who are likely to see a decrease in bone density with menopause.

•Ensure you are fulfilling your calorie needs target.

Energy is a general interest for older adults. Your actual calorie needs may differ based on body composition and lifestyle. But here are some calorie needs for age 60 and beyond. It will help you get energized in the right proportion.

For Men:

Not active: 2,000-2,200 calories

Moderately active: 2,200 to 2,400 calories

Very active: 2,400 to 2,600 calories

For women:

Not active: 1,600 calories

Moderately active: 1,800 calories

Very active: 2,000 to 2,200 calories

Remember, a healthy life is a wealthy life. You don't need to break boundaries to stay healthy and youthful as you age.

•Enjoy your favorite dark green veggies.

Calcium is very vital concerning the gone health and osteoporosis prevention.

What is Oestoporosis?

Osteoporosis is a condition in which bone density diminishes, thereby increasing the risk of falls and bone fractures. Calcium is additionally significant for muscle movement and blood circulation.

Dairy products such as cheese, yogurt, and milk are common sources of calcium. This supplement is also found in green vegetables like kale, broccoli, and bok choy. It's likewise fortified in some plant-based milk, oats, and orange juice.

Focus on your vitamin K levels

Vitamin K is significant for slowing the aging process since deficiency is connected to arthritis, cardiovascular diseases, and osteoporosis. This vitamin additionally plays a significant part in blood clotting or wound healing. It's significant for individuals who take blood-thinning medications to keep up with their vitamin K levels. A medical care provider can recommend what a healthy level looks like for you.

Vitamin K can be acquired from soybeans, pumpkin, veggies like turnip green, and broccoli.

When we talk about foods to eat we should also look at foods we shouldn't eat to promote healthy aging.

Focus on your health by taking nutritious balanced diets and consuming less salt, sugar, and saturated fats can go quite far in sound aging.

According to Sauceda, "Added sugar is probably the one thing across the board," and *"Reducing sugar intake can hugely impact heart health, blood sugar, and energy."*

Less intake of salt and opting for salt derivatives can assist with blood pressure levels. High blood pressure is a negative factor for heart disease.

Likewise, saturated fats can add to undesirable cholesterol levels. Eating more streamlined cuts of meat and reducing red meat consumption can assist you with lessening your cholesterol level.

Keep in mind, that a healthy life is a wealthy life.

Do things you love frequently

There's no such happiness as doing things you love doing. There is always a feeling of satisfaction/fulfillment whenever you make it happen.

Hobbies are important for people of all ages, everything being equal. Hobbies develop a beginner's mindset, a feeling of energy, and creativity. Our leisure activities, however, additionally have benefits for our prosperity.

Whether practicing yoga or learning a new language, remaining intellectually dynamic keeps us associated with what we love.

The National Institute of Aging says, "Engaging in coping mechanisms becomes interesting, engaging in activities as we age helps us develop healthy and more strong. "

Enjoy the honor of Aging.

Mark Twain frankly said, "Don't say anything negative about becoming old. It is an honor denied to many"

Unfortunately, we often do not consider it as grace from our maker, God. Furthermore, aging it's not without its difficulties but rather we ought to see becoming older as a gift. Also, it is something special to be admired and enjoyed.

Practice appreciation and encircle yourself with those close to you. Do things that you've always wanted to do or that make you blissful. Appreciate how you ended up — all things considered, you're the individual you couldn't wait to grow up to be. Appreciate each experience, utilize the most out of it, and be happy for each outcome.

Stop smoking and tobacco use. (Quit hard drugs)

If you use tobacco, smoke, or consume hard drugs. It will be ideal to drop the habit now since it will help you feel better right away and lessen the dangers of health issues that accompanies hard drugs regardless of whether you've been on it for quite a while

CHAPTER 3: Would You Say You Are Aging Great or You Are Worn Out?

As referenced in the past chapters, healthy aging is a blossoming process in one's life. However, the question is, would you say you are aging great or you are worn out? You ought to take a look at these signs to confirm your current aging process:

- ☐ You carve out an opportunity to learn new things.
- ☐ You tell the truth about your needs.
- ☐ You have a community.
- ☐ You focus on your physical health.
- ☐ You do things you enjoy.
- ☐ You converse with your primary care physician about the medications you take.
- ☐ You plan for the future.
- ☐ You are grateful for who you have become.
- ☐ You are not lonely and depressed all of the time.
- ☐ You don't shy away from discussing your progress and lapses.
- ☐ You are not using age as an excuse always
- ☐ You don't consider yourself to be a lesser version of your youthful self

On a scale of 12, if you fulfill not less than seven (7) out of the above recorded. Congrats, you are Aging wonderfully and well. I'm glad for your growth and you ought to be a guide to people in the future.

Other notable signs are:

- ☐ Healthy skin
- ☐ StrongEnergy and endurance
- ☐ Great memory and cognitive performance

Test 1: Is it possible to switch the signs of aging?

Indeed, it's impractical to return to the past completely, there are ways of unwinding or even reversing some signs of aging. This is conceivable by adopting the tips earlier mentioned in Chapter 2 which are a healthy lifestyle, eating a balanced diet, and exercising consistently. You can diminish the risk of chronic disease and work on your overall physical and psychological well-being.

Test 2:How can I accept my age ?

Being pleased with your age implies accepting yourself for what and who you are and being impressed with your life experiences.

Try not to be timid or frightened to show your wrinkles or gray hair, they are signs of a wonderful life well-lived. Concentrate on what you can do rather than what you can't, and don't compare yourself with others. Have confidence in your potential.

All in all, aging well is feasible, and it's not just about looking youthful. By keeping a positive attitude, healthy way of life, dynamic brain, strong relationships, and embracing your age, you can age gracefully and enjoy your golden years to the fullest. So, don't be scared of growing older - embrace it!

Becoming old isn't a state of denial or self-worthlessness. Try not to leave yourself broken down but instead age well. Many look to age yet a few are privileged to see their golden years by the will of God.

There is more to do till the very end. Welcome the fears, be honest with yourself, and look for help when required. And trust me it would be more amazing than your youthful years that's why it is called the golden years.

CHAPTER 4: Things To Do Till The Very End.

Tell somebody how dear he/she is to you

In our life's journey, we are continually contacted and upheld by people around us, be it friends, family, or associates.

Can you at any point recognize somebody who has made an impact in your life? Compose a letter to the person today and let him/her know how much he/she means to you. You can do this however many times as you need, for as many people as you like. You can send them beautiful text messages. Don't underestimate the power of good words.

Perform a benevolent deed without expecting anything in return:

Many of us are in many cases waiting to receive as opposed to give. However, for any relationship to work, there must be both giving and receiving from both ends.
If you often find yourself wondering why nobody is giving you what you need, what about working on gifting others first? The rest will follow. Perform a thoughtful deed to be remembered for genuinely.

Consider that favor somebody you know needs so much and you are capable of fulfilling it. Make it a reality for that individual and perceive how happy he/she wil be. Little things or favors also count.

Try and be impactful (Be a mentor)

Teaching is one of the widely compensating things we can do. Regardless of how old you are, regardless of whether you are in your adolescence, prime, or old age, you are always in the position to coach another person given you have what it takes to impact. Maybe somebody more youthful than you or somebody older can profit from a specific mastery you have.

Tutoring others is likewise an extraordinary way for you to foster yourself as well. The more you show others, the less likely you are to forget your skill. You become more amazing in what you do.

Many communities are always searching for volunteer mentors, so check inside your nearby local area programs for such open doors. At the same time, is there anybody you realize who can profit from being tutored by you? Stretch out your hand to help — who knows, it could be what he/she needs this moment!

You don't become a successful person or knowledgeable by how much you acquire however you become one by the number of lives you have influenced/impacted. This is the genuine definition of success.

Keep great family ties and connection:

Live your golden days with a decent connection with families and Companions. Life is excessively short to keep loathes and, hard feelings. Experience the last days with blissful memories and not hurt. If you somehow managed to bite the dust today, would people be happy
you are gone or would be miserable because your sort was uncommon?

Ponder and reflect on this often. You never knew where, when, and how your final gasp would be.

Last Synopsis

Taking everything into account, aging healthy is attainable, and it's not just about looking youthful. By keeping an uplifting perspective, a solid way of life, a dynamic brain, solid connections, and embracing your age, you can improve with age and enjoy your golden years without limit.

Along these lines, don't fear progressing in years - embrace it! It is called golden years!!!

If you have been missing out, you can still make the best of it. It's not past the stage of no return. Leave gerenotophobia in the past. It's not over until it is finished!!!